GODS, HEROES, AND MYTHOLOGY

GREEK GODS, HEROES, AND MYTHOLOGY

BY A. W. BUCKEY

CONTENT CONSULTANT
Richard P. Martin
Antony and Isabelle Raubitschek Professor in Classics
Stanford University

Cover image: Pegasus, a winged horse, is one of many fantastical creatures in Greek mythology.

Core Library
An Imprint of Abdo Publishing
abdobooks.com

abdocorelibrary.com

Published by Abdo Publishing, a division of ABDO, PO Box 398166, Minneapolis, Minnesota 55439.

Printed in China
092018
012019

THIS BOOK CONTAINS RECYCLED MATERIALS

Cover Photo: DeAgostini/Getty Images
Interior Photos: DeAgostini/Getty Images, 1, 8; Georgios Tsichlis/Shutterstock Images, 4–5; Peter Hermes Furian/Shutterstock Images, 10; Adolfo Bezzi/Electa/Mondadori Portfolio/Hulton Fine Art Collection/Getty Images, 12–13; Shutterstock Images, 16; NYPL/Science Source, 18, 23, 26; Fine Art Images/Heritage Images/Hulton Fine Art Collection/Getty Images, 20–21; George Rinhart/Corbis Historical/Getty Images, 25, 43; Timothy Harding/Shutterstock Images, 28–29; Fine Art Images/Heritage Images/Getty Images, 30, 36–37, 45

Editor: Marie Pearson
Series Designer: Ryan Gale

Library of Congress Control Number: 2018949763

Publisher's Cataloging-in-Publication Data

Names: Buckey, A. W., author.
Title: Greek gods, heroes, and mythology / by A.W. Buckey.
Description: Minneapolis, Minnesota : Abdo Publishing, 2019 | Series: Gods, heroes, and mythology | Includes online resources and index.
Identifiers: ISBN 9781532117824 (lib. bdg.) | ISBN 9781532170683 (ebook)
Subjects: LCSH: Greek mythology--Juvenile literature. | Greek gods--Juvenile literature. | Heroes--Juvenile literature.
Classification: DDC 292.13--dc23

CONTENTS

CHAPTER ONE

INTO THE LABYRINTH

King Minos was the rich and powerful ruler of the island of Crete. He was loved by the gods. And he was a little too used to getting everything he wanted.

One day, Minos was walking on the beach. It was a beautiful day, and he was feeling grateful to the gods for his happy life. He asked the gods for an animal. He wanted to kill it in honor of the gods. This was known as a sacrifice. Sacrifices made the gods happy. The sea god Poseidon heard Minos's request. The most beautiful bull Minos had ever seen appeared on the beach.

Ruins of ancient palaces can still be found on Crete today.

When Minos saw the amazing bull, he couldn't bring himself to kill it. Instead, he hid the bull to keep for himself. Minos sacrificed an ordinary bull for Poseidon. But Poseidon was a god. He noticed the difference.

Poseidon was angry at Minos's disrespect. Aphrodite, the goddess of love, was angry too. Together, the two gods planned revenge. Aphrodite put a spell on Pasiphae, Minos's wife. Soon, the queen had a child. The baby had a human body and a bull's head. He became known as the Minotaur, and as he grew, he began to eat people.

CRETE

Today, the island of Crete is part of Greece. Long ago, there was another culture on Crete. This culture was the Minoan civilization. It was named for King Minos. Crete was the location of another important event in Greek mythology. The god Zeus was born on Crete. Zeus later became the king of all the gods.

THE MINOTAUR AND THE LABYRINTH

King Minos was horrified. He had a complicated maze built inside his kingdom. He sent the Minotaur to live in the maze alone. This lonely puzzle of a home was called the Labyrinth.

King Minos used the Labyrinth for his own revenge. He was angry with the city of Athens, so he demanded a sacrifice from the city. Every nine years, Athens had to send him seven young men and seven young women. He sent these unlucky people to the Labyrinth. They met the Minotaur there and never came back.

This terrible tradition continued until the famous hero Theseus came to Crete. Heroes are the children of gods or kings. They go on adventures to achieve some special task. On the way, they face obstacles such as monsters and evil kings. Theseus entered the Labyrinth and killed the Minotaur. One of Minos's daughters, the clever Ariadne, helped him. The princess helped Theseus solve the puzzle of the maze. She gave him a

Ancient artwork depicts the story of Theseus killing the Minotaur.

ball of string. Theseus unspooled the string behind him so he never lost his place inside the Labyrinth.

ANCIENT GREEK MYTHS

The story of the Minotaur comes from the tradition of Greek mythology. The ancient Greeks were people who lived in what are now Greece, Turkey, and islands in the Mediterranean Sea. They lived in many different small cities that were separate kingdoms. Powerful Greek kingdoms also conquered land in Eastern Europe, Italy, Spain, and France. They spread their culture there. These people were connected by their language, ancient Greek. They also shared a common religion and culture. Ancient Greek culture flourished from around 1400 BCE to about 300 CE.

Greek religion was polytheistic. This means that the Greeks worshipped many gods. They built temples dedicated to their gods. They also worshipped them with rituals and sacrifices. The Greeks told stories about their gods. These stories helped explain who the gods were. They showed how gods and goddesses related to human beings. The Greeks also told stories about magical animals that lived in nature.

Greek stories were full of tales about famous heroes. Their adventures were full of war, romance,

MAP OF GREECE

This map shows the country of Greece as it appears today. Crete and Athens are marked on the map. In ancient times, Greek culture spread to other islands and all across Europe. Greek culture was especially powerful from about 800 to 300 BCE. Many Greek cities and towns were on islands in the Mediterranean Sea. Others were along the coastline. Based on this map, why do you think the sea was important to the Greeks?

and magic. The traditional stories of the ancient Greeks are called myths. Myths are stories that involve the gods and supernatural events. They are not always based on fact. However, myths can reveal truths that more realistic stories cannot.

ANCIENT GREEK ART

The ancient Greek people told their stories in many ways. Famous poets would recite them as long poems. One of these poets was Homer. He lived approximately 3,000 years ago, but his poetry is still famous today. The Greeks also told stories through paintings, statues, and pieces of pottery. They painted the stories of famous heroes around the sides of large pots. These pots were made out of clay. Today, historians study Greek art to learn more about Greek myths and ideas.

Greek myths have influenced the stories and ideas of other cultures. They survive today in common words and phrases, as well as parts of other myths and stories. Greek myths have a long and powerful history. They start with the beginning of the universe and the birth of the gods.

CHAPTER TWO

THE GODS AND GODDESSES

Greek myths say that at the beginning of time, there was only the Sky and the Earth. The two came together to make a generation of gods called Titans. The Titans were giant and powerful.

Two Titans, Cronus and Rhea, gave birth to several new gods. Cronus believed his children would try to overthrow him. He swallowed each of them after they were born. Zeus, the youngest, escaped when Rhea gave Cronus a stone to swallow instead of a child.

Zeus is often depicted as a fierce god wielding lightning bolts.

Zeus grew up and killed Cronus. He freed his swallowed brothers and sisters. Zeus defeated the Titans and became the king of the gods. These gods made their home on Mount Olympus. The twelve gods on Mount Olympus are called the Olympians.

PROMETHEUS

Prometheus was a kind and clever Titan. He took Zeus's side in the war between gods and Titans. Prometheus created human beings and wanted to help them. Once, Prometheus stole fire from the gods and gave it to humans. Fire allowed people to warm themselves, cook food, build new crafts, and do many other things. But Zeus was furious that Prometheus had stolen from him. As punishment, Zeus chained Prometheus to a rock so that an eagle could eat his liver every day. The liver grew back each night, meaning Prometheus would suffer forever.

THE OLYMPIANS

Zeus is a powerful sky god and the king of the Olympians. He is married to his sister Hera. Hera is the beautiful goddess of marriage. However, Zeus also has other relationships. This makes Hera very jealous. Demeter is another sister of Zeus.

She is the goddess of plants and farming. Their brother Hades is the god of the underworld. He is the ruler of the dead. Poseidon, their other brother, is the god of the sea. These children of Cronus have one last sister, Hestia. She is the goddess of the hearth, or home fire. She tends to the hearth in the main house at Olympus.

HADES AND PERSEPHONE

One myth explains why Earth has seasons. Hades wanted a wife. So he kidnapped Demeter's daughter Persephone. Demeter was so sad that she let all the crops die. Finally, Demeter convinced Hades to let Persephone come back to Earth. But there was a catch. Persephone had eaten some pomegranate seeds in the underworld. This meant she would always have to go to the underworld for part of the year. This is why the world has winter. During this time, Demeter misses her daughter. Plants do not grow.

Zeus and Hera's son is Ares. He is the cruel and violent god of war. Hera also has another son, Hephaestus. He is the god of fire and craftspeople. He can make beautiful things from metal. Aphrodite is the

gorgeous goddess of love. She was born out of sea foam. Aphrodite can make anyone fall in love, but she does not love her husband Hephaestus. The two are unhappily married.

The remaining Olympians are Zeus's children with other gods and humans. There are the twins Apollo and Artemis. Apollo is the handsome god of music, oracles, and marksmanship with the bow and arrow. Artemis is the goddess of wild things and hunting. Zeus's son Hermes is the quick and tricky messenger of the gods. Dionysus is a fun and charming god of wine. Athena is the goddess of reason and strategy. Some stories tell how Zeus swallowed Athena's mother, Metis, just as Zeus's father had tried to swallow him. Athena was born when she burst out of his head. Athena, Artemis, and Hestia all chose not to marry or have children.

Mount Olympus, Greece's highest peak, was a natural place for ancient Greeks to associate with the gods.

Apollo, *left*, and Artemis, *right*, are two of the children of Zeus.

THE OTHER GODS

There are dozens of other gods besides the Olympians. Most of the gods had children, and some of those children were gods also. Three women called Fates are very powerful. They are not quite goddesses, but they decide people's fate, or destiny. They spin life like woolen thread. One Fate spins the string of life. The second Fate measures how long it will be. And the third Fate decides when to cut it off at death.

STRAIGHT TO THE SOURCE

Hesiod was an ancient Greek poet from the 700s BCE. He wrote about how Zeus responded after he learned that Metis would give birth to a child wiser and more powerful than Zeus:

> *Zeus, therefore, swallowed Metis. . . . Metis, however, soon conceived Pallas Athena. And, furthermore, Metis, the mother of Athena, who was even wiser than the gods and mortal men, remained concealed within the innermost parts of Zeus. There the goddess Athena received from her father the aegis [shield], with which she surpassed in strength all the other immortal gods who have their dwellings on Olympus. [Zeus] brought her into the world, bearing the aegis and clad in the armor of war, from out of his head on the shores of Lake Tritonis.*

Source: Rhoda A. Hendricks. *Classical Gods and Heroes.* New York: Perennial, 2004. Print. 39.

Consider Your Audience

Review this passage closely. Consider how you would adapt it for a different audience, such as your parents or younger friends. Write a blog post conveying this same information for the new audience. What is the most effective way to get your point across to this audience? How does your new approach differ from the original text, and why?

CHAPTER THREE

NYMPHS, SATYRS, AND MAGICAL BEASTS

The Greeks believed that trees, rivers, and oceans were home to spirits. Greek myths are full of these spirits, as well as frightening monsters and beautiful, magical animals. They also spoke of some creatures that were part human and part animal.

NEREIDS, NAIADS, AND DRYADS

Nymphs are spirits of nature in Greek mythology. There are many different kinds.

In one story, Apollo falls in love with the naiad Daphne, and Daphne turns into a laurel tree.

Nereids and naiads are two types of water spirits. Nereids live throughout the sea, and naiads live in freshwater places. Each small river, pond, or pool has its own nymph. Dryads are similar to naiads and nereids. They are the spirits of trees. These nature spirits are described as beautiful young women. They sometimes married humans or gods. For example, the nereid Thetis married a human king. Her son was the famous Greek hero Achilles.

PAN

Pan is a god who is part animal and part human. He is a son of Hermes. Like many satyrs, he has a human head and upper body, and the legs, feet, and horns of a goat. Pan is a god of herders and loves to be out in nature. According to myths, he invented a musical pipe. Pan liked to scare people. When people heard eerie sounds in the woods, they thought he was trying to frighten them. The word *panic* comes from Pan's ability to surprise.

SATYRS AND CENTAURS

The Minotaur was not the only ancient Greek creature that was a mix of human and animal. Satyrs are men who are half goat. They love

The Greek god Pan is similar in appearance to a satyr.

to wander outside, have fun, and celebrate. Greek mythology also tells the story of the centaurs. They have the heads and torsos of human men and the bodies of horses. Centaurs are sons of King Ixion. Ixion was Ares's son. Ixion once insulted Zeus. As punishment, Ixion's sons were born as centaurs. Most centaurs are rude and wild. But one, Chiron, is calm and wise. Chiron practices medicine and helped raise two Greek heroes, Achilles and Jason.

MYTHICAL BEASTS

Several beasts and monsters show up in Greek myths. Many of these monsters are large and dangerous. Some have the power to kill human heroes. On land, there is the Chimera. This fearsome monster is a combination of a lion, a goat, and a giant snake. The Chimera lives in the eastern part of the Greek empire and attacks local people.

THE GODS AND THEIR ANIMALS

The Greek gods of Olympus had favorite animals. These animals would remind ancient Greeks of the god or goddess they worshipped. For example, Hera's favorite birds were peacocks and cuckoos. Apollo was the sun god and Poseidon was the sea god. One of Apollo's special animals is the dolphin. Poseidon's is the horse. Zeus was able to change into many different animals, including a swan, an eagle, and a bull.

In the ancient Greek story the *Odyssey,* Scylla attacks a ship and its crew.

In the Mediterranean Sea, sailors had to beware of Scylla and Charybdis. Scylla was once a beautiful nymph. Now she has twelve feet and several snake and dog heads. She uses them to eat sailors. She lives across a narrow passage from the whirlpool monster Charybdis.

Meanwhile, in the underworld, the dead have to pass by Cerberus. He is the three-headed dog who guards the way to Hades. Cerberus keeps living people

L'ANDROMEDA
ASCANIO PIO di SAVOIA

from entering Hades and stops dead people from leaving it. Some stories say he has snake heads on his back.

Not all magical beasts brought danger. Pegasus, a horse with wings, has magical powers and a gold harness. He helps a Greek hero slay the Chimera. Pegasus makes his home on Mount Olympus. There is also a flying ram with a magical golden fleece. This sheep once saved the life of a child by flying all the way across an ocean.

EXPLORE ONLINE

Chapter Three discusses the creatures of Greek mythology. The article at the website below gives more information on this topic. Does the article answer any of the questions you had about creatures in Greek mythology?

GREEK MYTHOLOGY'S MYSTICAL CREATURES

abdocorelibrary.com/greek-mythology

In Greek mythology, the winged horse Pegasus is caught by the hero Bellerophon near a fountain.

CHAPTER FOUR

PASSION, WAR, AND HEROES

The stories of Greek mythology have many twists and turns. But they contain similar ideas. One important idea in Greek myth is that love is a very powerful emotion. Aphrodite and the love god Eros can make any person fall in love in a single moment. These powerful feelings can cause people and gods to do extreme things.

Many Greek stories include tales of kings and war. These stories star heroes. True Greek heroes can sometimes be violent or dishonest, but they are always brave. The two most

The poet Homer is responsible for some of the best-known versions of Greek mythological tales.

famous ancient Greek epic poems are the *Iliad* and the *Odyssey*. They are both by the poet Homer. The *Iliad* is about the Trojan War. This was a war between the ancient Greeks and a city called Troy. The *Odyssey* is about one hero of the Trojan War and his long voyage home.

THE PASSION OF PARIS

The Trojan War began with an argument between the gods. Eris was the goddess of strife, or disagreement. She found a beautiful golden apple and wrote that it was for only the most beautiful goddess. Then she tossed the apple among a group of goddesses. Hera, Aphrodite, and Athena fought over it. They told Paris, a prince from the city of Troy, to choose who should get the apple. Paris chose Aphrodite, the goddess of love.

As a reward, Aphrodite promised Paris the most beautiful woman in the world. This was Helen, the Queen of Sparta, a city in Greece. Helen was already

In Homer's stories, Paris's actions trigger a war that goes on for many years and involves great cities, heroes, and gods.

married, but Paris didn't care. He sailed to Sparta and took Helen back to his city, Troy. The Greeks sailed after him to get her back.

Paris's passion for Helen caused a great war that lasted approximately ten years. The gods took sides and joined the fight. Hera and Athena were on the side of the Greeks. Aphrodite and Ares joined the Trojans. The Greeks fought hard to conquer Troy. However, they could not get past the city's high protective wall. Finally, the Greeks won by using a trick. They hid their soldiers inside a giant wooden horse and gave the horse as a gift to Troy. When the Trojans brought the horse inside their gates, the Greek soldiers sprang out and destroyed the city.

FAMOUS GREEK HEROES

Once the war was over, the Greeks journeyed home. Homer's epic poem the *Odyssey* tells of the Greek hero Odysseus. On the way home he faced many dangers, including the Cyclopes. The Cyclopes were one-eyed giants who lived in a cave on an island. When Odysseus and his men landed on the island, a Cyclops named Polyphemus started to eat the sailors.

Odysseus was clever. He told the Cyclops his name was "Nobody." Then Odysseus attacked Polyphemus. The giant cried out, "Nobody is hurting me!" None of the other Cyclopes came to help, and Odysseus was able to get away. But Polyphemus was the son of Poseidon, the sea god.

THE STRENGTH OF HERACLES

One of the most famous Greek heroes is Zeus's son Heracles, known for his incredible strength. When he was a young man, Heracles committed a terrible crime. As punishment, a king gave him a series of dangerous and difficult jobs, or labors. In one, Heracles had to go to Crete and steal King Minos's bull. In another, he had to get past a dragon and some nymphs to take golden apples, located at the far edge of the world, from Zeus. In the end, Heracles completed 12 labors. He became known as a great hero.

ANTIGONE

Some heroes were women. Antigone helped guide her blind father. After his death, she tried to make peace between her two brothers. Eteocles was king of Thebes. Polyneices attacked the city to try to win the throne. Both died in the struggle, and their uncle became king. Their uncle ordered that Polyneices's body be denied proper burial as punishment for betraying the crown. But Antigone still loved her brother, so she buried him. Her uncle ordered her to be killed.

Poseidon took his revenge and made the seas rough for Odysseus and his men.

Odysseus used all his smarts and courage to get from Troy to Greece. But the trip across the sea still took him several years. He was the only member of his crew who survived.

STRAIGHT TO THE SOURCE

The Greek historian Apollodorus wrote down the story of Heracles in *The Labors of Heracles.* He describes Heracles's final labor: going to Hades and stealing Cerberus, the guard dog of the underworld:

> *The twelfth labor [the king] set for him was to bring Cerberus from Hades. Cerberus had three dog-heads, a dragon's tail, and on his back he had the heads of all kinds of snakes. . . . When Heracles asked [Hades] for Cerberus, [Hades] told him to take him, if he could overpower him without the help of his weapons. Heracles found Cerberus at the gates of Acheron, and he threw his arms around his neck and did not loosen his strangle until the dog was subdued, even though he was bitten by the dragon in the dog's tail. Then he took the dog off with him and ascended to earth again.*

Source: Rhoda A. Hendricks. *Classical Gods and Heroes.* New York: Perennial, 2004. Print. 164–165.

What's the Big Idea?

Read the text carefully. What is the main idea of the passage? Write down two or three details in the passage that support this idea, and explain how they support it.

CHAPTER FIVE

GREEK MYTHS TODAY

Ancient Greek myths spread throughout Europe and the rest of the world. In the second and first centuries BCE, Roman invaders from Italy conquered the Greeks. The Romans admired Greek culture. They took on many gods and myths as their own. Then, the Roman Empire spread through western Europe and North Africa. In Eastern Europe, the Byzantine Empire spread Greek language and culture. During the European Renaissance from the 1500s through the 1700s, many artists and thinkers became interested in Greek myths again.

Greek mythology has been a popular subject of fine art for hundreds of years.

A CLASSICAL EDUCATION

The stories of ancient Greece were retold by the Romans in their language, Latin. Long after the Roman Empire fell, people continued to study Greek and Roman language and culture. The earliest universities in Europe taught ancient Greek and Latin texts as an important part of a classical education. Today, students who take classes in the classics study the same ancient stories.

LANGUAGE AND THOUGHT

There are traces of Greek myths in the way people talk and think today. For example, the word *odyssey* now means a long and tiring journey, just like the one Odysseus took. A *Trojan horse* is a name for something that seems harmless but hides something dangerous. Some computer viruses are called Trojan horses because they look like normal software. Once loaded onto a computer, they can cause great damage. The Olympic Games are named after ancient Greek games held to honor Zeus. Some people still use the

GREEK MYTHOLOGY IN ENGLISH SAYINGS

References to Greek mythology live on in many sayings that are common in English today. Why do you think tales from Greek mythology have survived for so long? Have you ever heard any of these expressions in your daily life?

Saying: Herculean task

Meaning: A difficult job

Reference: The 12 labors of Heracles (known as Hercules in ancient Rome)

Saying: Achilles's heel

Meaning: A person's one weakness

Reference: A powerful hero of the Trojan War, Achilles, whose one weak point was on his heel

Saying: The Midas touch

Meaning: The ability to succeed in business or other money matters

Reference: King Midas, who received a curse that caused everything he touched to turn to gold

word *Hades* to mean the world of the dead. A strong and powerful person is often known as a *titan*. And a complicated maze is still called a *labyrinth*.

ASTRONOMY AND GREEK MYTHOLOGY

The ancient Greeks paid close attention to the stars. The word *astronomy* comes from the ancient Greek word for "star-arranging." Many constellations, or groups of stars, have stories in Greek mythology that explain where they come from. For example, the constellation Centaurus is named after the centaur Chiron. The myths tell how after Chiron died, the gods made him into a pattern of stars in the sky.

GREEK MYTHOLOGY TODAY

Greek mythology can be found in modern books, movies, and video games. Rick Riordan's Percy Jackson and the Olympians series tells the stories of Greek gods in the present day. In Riordan's version, Athena studies military history and Ares rides a motorcycle. Disney made a movie called *Hercules* that borrows from the Hercules myth. The video game series God of War is set in the world of ancient Greek myths.

Greek myths can pop up in unexpected places. A three-headed dog similar to Cerberus appears in *Harry Potter and the Sorcerer's Stone*. In this book, the dog's name is Fluffy. These ancient stories from Greece continue to live on in our thoughts, our words, and our imaginations today.

FURTHER EVIDENCE

Chapter Five discusses Greek mythology in the world today. What is the main idea of the chapter? What evidence from the chapter supports this idea? Visit the website below to watch the trailer for *Percy Jackson: Sea of Monsters*. Does this trailer support the main idea of the chapter? Does it present new evidence?

PERCY JACKSON: SEA OF MONSTERS

abdocorelibrary.com/greek-mythology

FAST FACTS

Gods and Goddesses

- Aphrodite is the goddess of love.
- Apollo is the god of music and marksmanship. His twin, Artemis, is the goddess of wild things and hunting.
- Ares is the god of war.
- Athena is Zeus's daughter and the goddess of reason and wisdom.
- Hades is the god of the underworld. The underworld is also named after him.
- Hera is Zeus's wife and the goddess of marriage.
- Zeus is the sky god and the king of the gods.

Creatures

- Cerberus is the three-headed dog that guards the way to Hades.
- Naiads and nereids are the spirits of bodies of water. Dryads are the spirits of trees.
- Pegasus is a magical winged horse that can fly to Mount Olympus.
- Scylla is a multi-headed monster and Charybdis is a sea monster.

Stories

- The story of the Minotaur starts with King Minos, who was punished for not sacrificing the bull Poseidon gifted him. Poseidon cursed Minos's wife so she gave birth to a child with a bull's head. They called him the Minotaur and put him in a maze called the Labyrinth.
- The *Iliad* tells the story of the Trojan War. The human prince Paris stole the most beautiful woman in the world, Helen. He brought her back to Troy. This started a long war between the Greeks and the Trojans.
- The *Odyssey* tells of Odysseus's dangerous journey from Troy back to Greece. The trip took him many years and included adventures and losses.

STOP AND THINK

Why Do I Care?

The ancient Greeks lived a very long time ago. Why do you think that some people study Greek myths today? What kinds of things can we learn from studying the history and stories of ancient Greece?

Take a Stand

Some gods took Greece's side in in the Trojan War. They felt that it was unfair that Paris took Helen from a Greek king. Others sympathized with Paris and Troy. They didn't want the Trojan people to suffer for what Paris had done. Do you think the Greeks were right to attack Troy? Or should they have tried to solve the disagreement another way? Why?

You Are There

Chapter Four tells the story of Odysseus's trip home after the war. Imagine you are a member of Odysseus's crew. Write a letter to your friends at home. What has the trip been like for you?

Dig Deeper

After reading this book, what questions do you still have about Greek mythology? With an adult's help, find a few reliable sources that can help you answer your questions. Write a paragraph about what you learned.

GLOSSARY

charming
attractive and pleasing

classics
the study of the language and culture of ancient Greece and Rome

craftspeople
people who have a special skill for making things

culture
beliefs, art, language, and other customs shared by a group of people

epic poem
a long poem that tells a story, often involving the adventures of a hero

hero
in Greek mythology, a hero is a brave person who goes on adventures

oracle
a person who can foresee the future

polytheism
belief in many gods

sacrifice
a gift to a god or goddess

spirit
a supernatural being that dwells in a natural object, such as a tree or body of water

supernatural
beings and events that do not follow the laws of nature

ONLINE RESOURCES

To learn more about Greek gods, heroes, and mythology, visit our free resource websites below.

Core Library CONNECTION
FREE! COMMON CORE MULTIMEDIA RESOURCES

Visit **abdocorelibrary.com** for free Common Core resources for teachers and students, including vetted activities, multimedia, and booklinks, for deeper subject comprehension.

Booklinks NONFICTION NETWORK
FREE! ONLINE NONFICTION RESOURCES

Visit **abdobooklinks.com** for free additional online weblinks for further learning. These links are routinely monitored and updated to provide the most current information available.

LEARN MORE

Higgins, Melissa. *Sea Monsters*. Minneapolis, MN: Abdo, 2014.

Sherman, Patrice. *Roman Gods, Heroes, and Mythology*. Minneapolis, MN: Abdo, 2019.

INDEX

About the Author

A. W. Buckey is a writer and tutor living in Brooklyn, New York.